THE SUSTAINABLE
HOME

THE SUSTAINABLE
HOME

EASY WAYS TO LIVE WITH NATURE IN MIND

TEXT, PHOTOGRAPHY AND DESIGN

Ida Magntorn

PAVILION

CONTENTS

INTRODUCTION 7

THE EARTH'S RESOURCES 11

A CIRCULAR ECONOMY 17

THE KITCHEN 18
Eco-boost the kitchen 24
New kitchen? 27
Eat less meat 32
A plastic diet 41
When you feel inspired 51

THE BEDROOM 53
Eco-boost the bedroom 55
Easy to clean 58
Sheets – old is best 62
When you feel inspired 66
A good night's sleep 69

THE WARDROBE 70
Eco-boost the laundry 72
When you feel inspired 75

HOUSE PLANTS 77
Clean air 78
Cuttings 83

THE LIVING ROOM 85
Crystal chandelier or slide? 86
Eco-boost the living room 88
New sofa? 92
My second-hand sofas 95
When you feel inspired 98

LIGHTING 105
LED and incandescent light bulbs 106
Light sources 109
How many lights? 111
Candles 112
When you feel inspired 113

FLOWERS 114
Think like a florist 118
The top flowers 121
Homemade eco-friendly plant food 122
When you feel inspired 125

THE BATHROOM 127
Eco-friendly bathroom dreams 128
Bath vs shower 129
When you feel inspired 130

CLEANING 132
Natural cleaning 134
Homemade cleaning solutions 135

STUFF 136
A new style 138
Second hand 139

FURTHER READING 142

PICTURE CREDITS 143

ACKNOWLEDGEMENTS 144

INTRODUCTION

How can you create a home that is good for the environment, sustainable in the long run and at the same time harmonious, individual, exciting and interesting?

We all know the score – we live beyond the earth's means. The current total population of the world would need the resources of 1.7 earths, and in the UK the equivalent of 2.7 earths, to cover what we consume. Using less of nature's resources and limiting emissions of carbon dioxide are essential for the planet to be habitable in the future.

Now, this may sound bleak and difficult, but there are many ways we can contribute to turning the tide. In this book, I focus on how we can adopt an eco-friendly approach when we decorate, partly by using examples from my own home, and partly by looking at tips from others – everything from reusing what you already have and clever flea market finds to making bouquets from locally grown flowers, cleaning in an eco-friendly way and making your home more energy-efficient. You will also get tips on how to go on a plastic diet, which lighting is the best and how to choose a climate-smart mattress. The big and the small side by side, in other words.

In a practical sense, this approach builds on the expression *reduce, reuse, recycle* (as opposed to buy, use, throw away). In the long run it's about aiming for a fully circular economy: to recycle, mend and regard what's intended to be thrown away as a resource. Read more about the circular economy on page 17.

When you decorate a completely new home, or when you just feel like making small changes and perhaps buying something extra, it's time to stop and consider. Perhaps you can try rearranging furniture you already have, or see if you own things that you can alter or freshen up? Make something new from something old. And if you really don't find what you need at home, see if you can buy it second hand. Either you can look for something to use just as it is, or find an object that, with some work, can be transformed into something else.

Reduce, reuse, recycle

THINGS TO CONSIDER
when you want to decorate in an eco-friendly way:

USE WHAT YOU'VE GOT. It doesn't matter how eco-friendly your new kitchen is if it has replaced one that was still in working order.

IF YOU'RE TIRED of what you've got, think about whether you can remake, paint or perhaps transform an object into something completely different.

BUY SECOND HAND if you absolutely have to buy something.

LOOK FOR PRODUCTS THAT CAN BE RECYCLED – solid wood instead of veneer, for example. The easier a piece of furniture is to sand down or remake, the more likely it is to be a long-term purchase. And don't forget to recycle!

IF YOU REALLY CAN'T FIND ANYTHING SECOND HAND, go for design classics when you buy new. They are usually of superior quality and therefore also have a high second-hand value. Also keep in mind that most design classics can actually be found second hand. Look around at some auction sites; see tips on page 139.

IF YOU STILL CHOOSE TO BUY NEW, go for eco-labelled items if you can. Find out which components in the product the certification refers to.

TAKE CARE OF WHAT YOU'VE GOT. By looking after your furniture and other possessions, you will extend their lives and save the energy and materials that would have been used to produce replacements. Plus you won't contribute to the rubbish mountain.

Before we further explore eco-friendly design room by room, it is helpful to look at a bit of background and terminology relating to the earth's resources.

THE EARTH'S RESOURCES

The global average temperature is rising due to large emissions of greenhouse gases, in particular carbon dioxide. Environmental damage is everywhere. When it comes to our homes, it is caused by everything from how our furniture is produced and transported to things that might not always spring to mind, such as how your Friday bouquet of flowers has been cultivated.

YOUR ECOLOGICAL FOOTPRINT is the impact that your behaviour and consumption have on the earth's resources. In the UK we emit on average approximately 12.7 tonnes of carbon dioxide per person per year. We need to do all we can to bring this under 1 tonne to limit global warming.

Calculate your own ecological footprint:
footprint.wwf.org.uk
footprintnetwork.org
footprintcalculator.org

HOW MUCH IS A KILO OF
CARBON DIOXIDE?

It's very easy to end up talking in numbers and comparisons when you want to get to grips with the breadth of the climate issue. To help you visualize how much 1 kilo of carbon dioxide is, think like this: 1 kilo of lead of course weighs the same as 1 kilo of cotton. But cotton takes up a much larger area since lead is more dense. Carbon dioxide, on the other hand, is less dense than cotton. 1 kilo of carbon dioxide takes up 0.5 cubic metres, which is about the equivalent of three bathtubs.

However, it can be useful to remember that everything is relative, and numbers that might sound sky high can in fact be fairly low when seen from a different perspective. Here's an example:

PARAFFIN VS STEARIN

If we consistently swapped the climate-damaging paraffin candle for candles made from stearin, it would cut our carbon emissions by the same amount as if we removed 15,000 petrol cars from the roads. That is as many cars as are in Newquay in Cornwall, which might seem like a lot until you realize that 15,000 cars constitute just 0.0004 per cent of the UK's total of 32.6 million cars. The same saving would be achieved if petrol consumption was reduced by around 2 litres for each car per year. So perhaps it isn't that much after all? But as the old saying goes, every little helps.

The World Wildlife Fund for Nature has neatly summarized the most important issues around carbon emissions in five points. These can be useful to keep in mind to become more climate smart.

THE FIVE POINTS

TRAVEL – Covers travel and transport. Prioritize the bicycle over the car and the train over the plane.
FOOD – Covers what we eat. Choose more vegetarian options. Reduce food waste; don't let food or leftovers go in the bin.
HOME – Covers energy consumption. Choose green electricity and heating. Live in a smaller space.
STOCKS – Covers how money is managed and invested. Aim for ethical and green savings and pensions; avoid funds that are linked to oil, gas or coal companies, for example.
STUFF – Covers consumption. Buy fewer new goods and use circular and digital services.

SOME IMPORTANT INITIATIVES

EARTH OVERSHOOT DAY is the day of the year when we have used up the equivalent resources that the earth can regenerate in one year – that is, the day on which we start to live beyond our means. Due to our impact on the climate, this day falls earlier and earlier. The way this is calculated is becoming ever more sophisticated and the dates are adjusted every year, but it is clear that since the start of the 1970s Earth Overshoot Day has moved forward from December to July.

EARTH HOUR was established in Australia in 2007 to bring attention to climate and energy issues. Every year on the last Saturday in March, all lights are switched off for an hour. In 2019, 188 countries all over the world participated, and lights were switched off in private homes and public buildings such as the Sydney Opera House, the Empire State Building in New York and the Eiffel Tower in Paris.

THE 2030 AGENDA comprises the United Nations' 17 global goals that were formulated in 2015 by world leaders to achieve a common sustainable development on every level – environmental, economic and social. It aims to eradicate extreme poverty and reduce inequality and injustice in the world, as well as solve the climate crisis.

THE PARIS AGREEMENT was signed at the UN's climate conference held in that city in 2015. It is an agreement between the countries of the world to work together to prevent the earth's average temperature rising more than 2°C, ideally not more than 1.5°C. The first time we were able to measure the earth's average temperature was in 1850, when it was calculated at 13.6°C. Since then, the temperature has risen by almost a whole degree.

FRIDAYS FOR FUTURE is a global movement founded by Greta Thunberg in 2018. Thunberg sat in protest outside the parliament in Stockholm to call attention to the climate issue ahead of the general election that autumn. Since then, schoolchildren and students in over 100 countries, on all continents, have been striking every Friday to get the politicians to adhere to the Paris Agreement.

Linear economy – 'take, make, dispose'
Circular economy – 'reduce, reuse, recycle'

A CIRCULAR ECONOMY

A circular economy is about actively working not to deplete
the earth's natural resources but instead to reuse what has been
used already. To make more from less, in other words – to reuse,
mend and regard things that were destined to be thrown away
as a resource.

You can envisage a circular economy as running parallel with
nature's cycle. Materials should either be biodegradable, so that they
disappear once they've been consumed, or function in a technical
cycle – reduce, reuse, recycle.

IT'S THE RESULT WE'RE AFTER

A circular economy also means that you don't have to own
everything you use. Sometimes you can rent or borrow. Consider
the new concept of a 'collaborative economy', which is about sharing
ownership more – starting to see consumers as users, and products
as functions.

Often, it's not the ownership of an object but its actual function
that we're after. A classic example is the communal laundry. The
laundry must be washed: it's the practical result that you need, not
the machine itself.

Sharing things also comes with other benefits, such as relationships
with the people you share them with. My friend used to live in a
block of flats with communal showers in the basement. While she
thinks it's nice to have her own shower nowadays, she sometimes
misses the everyday relationship that you develop with your
neighbours if you meet them in a dressing gown from time to time.

A COLLABORATIVE ECONOMY

By sharing ownership and helping each other out, we can save a
lot. Those who rent a holiday home for a couple of weeks instead of
owning it don't have to worry about renovations and other costs, and
the owner in turn gets money towards maintenance.

*'In contrast to the "take-make-waste" linear model, a circular economy is
regenerative by design and aims to gradually decouple growth from the
consumption of finite resources.'*

Ellen MacArthur Foundation

THE KITCHEN

the heart of the home

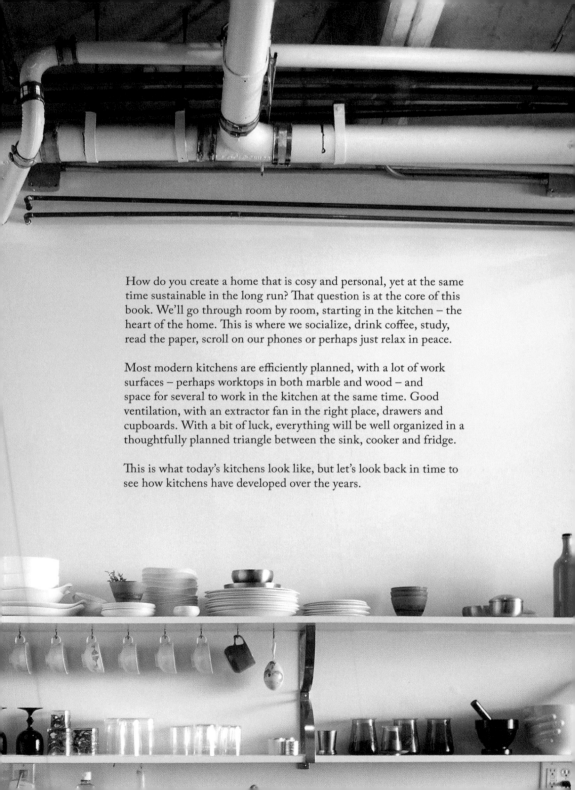

How do you create a home that is cosy and personal, yet at the same time sustainable in the long run? That question is at the core of this book. We'll go through room by room, starting in the kitchen – the heart of the home. This is where we socialize, drink coffee, study, read the paper, scroll on our phones or perhaps just relax in peace.

Most modern kitchens are efficiently planned, with a lot of work surfaces – perhaps worktops in both marble and wood – and space for several to work in the kitchen at the same time. Good ventilation, with an extractor fan in the right place, drawers and cupboards. With a bit of luck, everything will be well organized in a thoughtfully planned triangle between the sink, cooker and fridge.

This is what today's kitchens look like, but let's look back in time to see how kitchens have developed over the years.

A BRIEF HISTORY OF THE KITCHEN

Around the turn of the twentieth century, amid increasing industrialization, many people left the countryside to work in the city. People moved to small back-to-back or terraced houses, or multistorey tenements containing dark, cramped flats. Kitchens were small; there might have been a single bedroom and perhaps a parlour that no one dared use, which would sit unheated and preferably untouched. This wouldn't be referred to as a living room – a term that explicitly states that the room is intended to be lived in – until well into the twentieth century. Families were often large, and people had to sleep wherever they would fit, so there might be a pull-out bed in the kitchen. In the evening, you'd pile up all the furniture in one corner of the kitchen in order to pull out the bed and set it up for the night. It was cramped.

FUNCTIONALISM

Functionalism emerged during the interwar period in an attempt to solve the space issues. The number of steps required to go between the cooker, cupboard and dining table was measured and the results used when planning new housing. The ideal was a small, functional kitchen with easily maintained surfaces. No mess or stuff and modern food, preferably just tins to heat up. The results were, how should I put it, technical. The kitchen was still cramped, planned by someone who probably hadn't set foot in one since childhood. And the idea behind tinned food was that meals should be fixed quickly and easily – socializing would take place in other rooms. Designers hardly thought, as we do today, that where the food is prepared is where life happens. Nor that tinned food was expensive and few could afford it.

POSTWAR INTERIOR DECORATION

The response to dark and too-small homes eventually led to bright and light, easily moved furniture, and simplicity. Out went dark, heavy furniture and bold-patterned wallpaper, and in came light Windsor-style chairs and neat tables. Rooms should be well ventilated, and above all no one should sleep in the kitchen.

But living is about more than just practical solutions. 'You want the rosebud and the magic of the light too', writes Lena Larsson, one of the very first interior design consultants, in her book *Varje människa är ett skåp* (Every Person is a Cabinet). And some of the cosiness and comfort certainly disappeared in all the rationalization.

Back to today's often fairly well-organized kitchens and homes. Here we should pause a moment to think about rosebuds and how the light falls, don't you think? But most important of all, we should take time to consider how we can make our homes eco-friendly.

… easily moved furniture, simplicity

ECO-BOOST THE KITCHEN
Eight simple steps

COOKING

• Only boil the quantity of water in a kettle that you actually need.
• Always keep lids on pans when cooking.
• Check the temperature of your fridge and freezer (see page 30).

WASHING-UP

• Only run the dishwasher once it's full.
• Use eco-friendly detergent.
• Reuse your cloths, and clean sponge cloths in the dishwasher from time to time. Using linen cloths is best for the environment. Put them through the washing machine at 60°C minimum.

PLASTICS

• Go on a plastic diet! Swap plastic for glass, porcelain, wood or steel (see page 41).

WASTE

• Devise a clever system for sorting your waste, the easier the better.

It's much better to run a full dishwasher occasionally than to wash up by hand, even if you rinse the plates before putting them in the dishwasher, mainly because you will use less hot water. Washing up by hand consumes three to four times more energy.

A modern Grade A dishwasher uses 10–15 litres of water per cycle, depending on the programme. Calculations show that you would need more than 100 litres of water to do the same amount of washing-up by hand.

NEW KITCHEN?
Consider this:

THROWING OUT an existing kitchen is the absolute worst thing to do from an environmental perspective. Don't! It's almost always possible to fix up the kitchen that you've already got.

IS IT SUPER WORN? In most cases new paint is enough to revive it. Or perhaps replace the cupboard doors. If you do this, swap them for doors that are produced with the environment in mind.

LOOK FOR A FRAMEWORK made from recycled wood. IKEA sells cupboard doors made from recycled wood, with a finish made from old PET bottles.

IF YOU ABSOLUTELY must replace it, try to find a whole kitchen second hand.

WHATEVER YOU CHOOSE, avoid materials that can't be repaired, such as particle board, MDF and laminate.

IS THE WORKTOP TOO LOW? Raise it with a thick overlay or chopping board to get it to an ergonomic height instead of ripping it out.

IF YOU ARE REPLACING YOUR MIXER TAP, choose one that is water-saving.

AIM FOR EASY WASTE SORTING. The simpler this is to manage, the better chance that it will work well (see page 47).

MAJOR APPLIANCES
Fridge and freezer

Worth replacing, on the other hand, are the major appliances. These are continuously improving and becoming more efficient and will therefore use less electricity. Since the fridge and freezer are left on 24/7, their energy consumption is especially important. What's more, the appliance will soon pay for itself, for the same reason.

Today, a new fridge/freezer uses half the amount of energy of one made ten years ago. Fifteen years ago, the same combination would use three times more electricity than today. It's therefore good to keep the major appliances fairly up to date.

SIX CLEVER TIPS

KEEP THE TEMPERATURE about 5°C in the fridge and about -18°C in the freezer. Every degree colder in the freezer will increase energy consumption by 5 per cent.

VACUUM BEHIND the fridge and freezer. This prevents dust trapping heat, meaning the compressors work more efficiently and use less energy. If it's really dusty you can save as much as 20 per cent in energy consumption.

MAKE SURE YOUR FRIDGE AND FREEZER don't stand in direct sunlight, so they don't have to compensate for the heat generated by the sun. For the same reason, it's helpful if the fridge doesn't stand right next to the cooker.

THE EVAPORATOR COILS in the freezer will perform better if they are not coated in ice. Take the opportunity to defrost it when it's cold outside.

MAKE SURE THAT FOOD has cooled down before you put it in the fridge or freezer. Freeze food in flat parcels so it will both freeze and defrost quicker.

ARE YOU ARE LUCKY ENOUGH to have a pantry? Use it for vegetables that only need to be kept slightly cool and you will save a lot of space – it might be possible to have a smaller fridge.

THE PANTRY
and other clever stuff

When I lived in student halls in Paris, everyone used the same trick: since we didn't have a fridge, we filled a bag with everything that had to be stored cold and hung it out of the window. Clever, but perhaps not very pleasing to the eye, and you probably wouldn't be able to fit in a whole family's worth of produce (unless you put a bag in every window?).

I would love to have a classic pantry at home. One like my grandmother had, which you can walk in and out of and is cleverly planned with deeper shelves at the bottom and shallower shelves at the top so you get a nice overview.

Another clever feature from the past is glass containers for storing basic dry ingredients, which were fitted underneath wall-mounted kitchen cupboards. You can, of course, just as well use jars on a shelf or in a cupboard, but the nifty thing is having a designated place for basic ingredients that means you can avoid packaging and, in turn, reduce your waste.

Zero waste is originally an American idea, and is about living a life with less waste and with the aim of not generating any waste at all. The idea is summarized in five words, all beginning with the letter R:
Reduce, Reuse, Recycle (see page 7).
Refuse – that is, to refuse packaging.
Rot – to compost.

Products sold in bulk, without packaging, are already available in a lot of places. But packaging isn't always bad; the fact is that today's food waste has a bigger impact on the environment than the plastic that the food is packaged in. For example, a cucumber that is not wrapped in plastic will rot quicker and get thrown away, which is more damaging to the environment than the production of the plastic would have been.

One form of packaging that is super easy to do without is the plastic bottle of shop-bought water. In the United States, 1,500 plastic bottles are sold every second. Yes, you read that correctly, every second! Here in Northern Europe, we get perfect drinking water straight from the tap, so there is no need to buy it in bottles, which are usually made from plastic. If you want fizzy water, it's better to buy a carbonator and do it yourself.

EAT LESS MEAT

In the long run, simply going vegetarian every other day isn't going to cut it – we need more vegetables and less meat in our diets than that. To give a better overview, the WWF and One Planet Plate have put together a climate budget that shows we can each use 11 grams of carbon dioxide a week on food production if we are to reach the goal of not exceeding a 1.5°C rise in global temperature. This might be a bit difficult to comprehend, so they have also made up a weekly menu that you can use to keep within the limits. It includes one meat dish, one fish dish, one dish of mussels and the rest vegetarian. By using the WWF's food calculator, you can see the quantity of emissions your meal produces.

When it comes to biodiversity, we still need grazing animals, so it can be justifiable to eat a small amount of meat. When you do, it's important that the meat comes from pasture-fed animals. Game is a safe bet, but other certified pasture-fed meat can be found. Meat from game has a low climate impact and is better for our health. Animals that live in the wild don't eat dry feed and so have not been given the antibiotics that usually come with farming. Moreover, the meat is locally produced and seasonal.

REVERSING COUNTERURBANIZATION

Reversing counterurbanization – an exodus from urban to rural areas – is great for the climate, but how does it work in practice? It means moving to the city to avoid commuting by car, but still growing your own veg. In the best of worlds, you'd live in a small space, in a flat in the city, and within cycling distance of an allotment where you'd grow your own food. Or perhaps you would grow produce on your balcony or roof, or in a pallet outside. You can also grow vegetables inside – for example, tomatoes in a south-facing window in summer.

Why is biodiversity so important?
Because the more species there are in nature, the more able it will be to fight extreme weather and climate change.

GROW YOUR OWN AT HOME
Growing tomatoes:

• Use a long, narrow wooden crate. Line it with a plastic sheet so the water doesn't escape. Cover the base with clay pebbles and fill with compost.
• Sow tomato seeds in the box.
• Tie heavy-duty rope around the box, then attach the rope to the ceiling using hooks.
• Tie some string between the hooks in the ceiling, then tie thinner string on to that for the tomatoes to climb. Attach the thin string to the box with bulldog clips.
• Water sufficiently from time to time and wait for your first tomato harvest!

Don't panic if you don't have a spare wall for the plants to climb up — you actually just need a warm, light place.

Super simple green shoots!

Put a sheet of kitchen roll on a plate. Moisten it with water using a spray bottle. Sprinkle with seeds such as alfalfa, buckwheat, lentil or mung bean and spray again. If you want to create a bit of humidity, you can cover with a bell jar, but it's not essential — just make sure to keep the plate evenly moist. After just a day or two, the seeds will start sprouting. Now you should place them on the windowsill so that they get a lot of light. After around a week, it's time to harvest.

Pick and eat just the green shoots. Sprouted seeds are actually even quicker, but won't give as much greenery and the whole sprouting seed is consumed.
• Place seeds such as quinoa, cress, mustard or radish in a colander or sieve. Rinse them and soak in cold water overnight.
• Rinse the seeds thoroughly in the colander and place it over a bowl. Cover with a towel and rinse twice a day.
• You can also sprout the seeds in the same way using a jar, with a nylon sock for a lid. Place the jar upside down and tilted, on a drying rack for example, so the water can drain off.
• It will be ready within a week. Some varieties, such as white quinoa, will be ready in just 24 hours!

Why should you grow shoots and sprouts?
1. It's nice to see something sprouting in the darkness of winter.
2. By letting the seeds sprout instead of eating them dry, the minerals they contain will be easier for the body to absorb. Double the benefit, in other words.

ON EGGS

This nice little story comes from a friend who lives in the Swedish countryside.

'This summer we built a chicken and rabbit house from an old shed that stood empty in the garden. Never did I imagine that something so small would give us so much. Every morning before school, the kids go out and feed the chickens with our leftovers. When they come home in the afternoon they go straight there again, cuddle the animals a little and bring back beautiful, pastel-coloured eggs. From these, I make pancakes that we eat with cloudberry jam. Could it be more sustainable?'

Keeping your own chickens is, of course, also possible in smaller gardens in the city. If your neighbours will allow it, you can also get a cockerel.

A SATURDAY RITUAL

As you probably know, new habits need to be ingrained. Therefore, it's a good idea to mix up big changes with some cosy and simple ones too. Here's a good Saturday ritual for those who are able: cycle to the nearest greengrocer with as big a basket as you can manage. Fill it! Preferably to last you the whole week.

Which vegetables are best from an environmental perspective?
Generally, robust and hardy vegetables, such as:
• Root vegetables
• White cabbage
• Cauliflower
• Onion

Why?
1. These varieties are almost always cultivated on open land and will therefore have a lower impact on the climate than vegetables grown in a greenhouse.
2. They can be stored for a long time, which means that there is less waste both in the shops and at home.

Be climate smart: Eat vegetables, fruit and berries when they are in season. Then they will be at their peak quality and cheapest, and will require the least amount of energy to grow.

In the UK we throw away approximately 7 million tonnes of food every year. This waste – of food that is fully edible (not including peel, bones, etc.) and yet is still thrown away – is approximately 74 kilos per person per year. That means an average family with children throws away food worth £700 every year. Needless to say, the emissions created by wasted food add to the production of greenhouse gases.

Why do we throw so much away?
• We buy too much food.
• We fill the fridge and forget what we've put at the back.
• We are bad at eating up leftovers.

What can we do about it?
• Plan your shopping. Buy what's needed, no more.
• Keep track of what you've got at home.
• Store correctly.
• Don't throw food away just because it has passed its best-before date – often it will keep for much longer. Look, smell and taste first.
• Make use of leftovers: fill a lunchbox that you can take to work, freeze or use the leftovers in a new dish.

MOMENT OF CALM

In general, I think if we put more care into a meal, cook the food slowly, set the table nicely, make sure that everyone is at home for dinner and then enjoy it, we would probably end up with less waste as we would be more careful with the food. If you invest many hours in getting together for mealtimes you will also prepare better. Of course, it can be difficult to come together over food when we're busy with various evening activities – but perhaps it is worth a try?

A simple tip: Light a stearin candle for the table. In some ways, it almost automatically makes the meal last a little longer. One step closer to slow living and less food waste.

A PLASTIC DIET

What does it mean to go on a plastic diet? How do you do it? Why? There are two important aspects. The first one is about you – plastic is bad for our health. The second is about the environment – plastic causes a lot of harm to our planet. It's not, however, as straightforward as all plastic being bad and having to get rid of all of it. But almost …

A lot of plastic is made from non-renewable crude oil. When the oil is gone, it's gone, simple as that. Bioplastics, on the other hand, are made from substances such as cellulose, sugar cane or corn, which are constantly renewed. Bioplastics haven't got as many areas of application; they cannot, for example, replace crude oil plastics in computers or for some medical uses. Some plastics, on the other hand, are super easy to replace, such as bottles and containers.

It takes 450 years for a plastic bottle that has ended up in the natural environment to break down. By handing it in for recycling it can instead become a cork, a washing-up brush or a fence.

SOFT AND HARD

Plastic is made up of a blend of different additives depending on how it will be used. Several of the additives in plastic are both hormone-disrupting and carcinogenic. To explain the components of plastic in a simple way, compare it with bread: different combinations of ingredients will give the bread different qualities, and it can be rustic, fine, soft or crusty.

All soft plastic can be incinerated, and if it's done the correct way in an approved facility it becomes a good source of energy. From an environmental perspective, non-decomposable hard plastic is the big culprit. The fact that it won't decompose is a much greater problem than its being made from non-renewable resources. (Actually, only 4 per cent of all crude oil is made into plastic – the rest is mainly used for fuel.)

ADDITIVES

Unfortunately, plastic doesn't come with a list of ingredients, so we can't know exactly what is in each type. We can say that hard plastic is generally better from a health perspective than soft, since it contains fewer additives. Some important qualities that we want to benefit from almost always come with harmful substances included. And it's a blend of these that make the plastic:

• NON-FLAMMABLE
(used in electric cables and plastic in electronics)

• ANTIBACTERIAL
(used in shoes and sports clothes)

• DIRT AND WATER REPELLENT
(used in Teflon frying pans, polyamide frying utensils, takeaway cartons, furniture with textile upholstery)

• SOFTNESS
(used in certain toys and inflatable rubber rings)

We ingest these harmful additives in different ways, sometimes even just by breathing. Therefore, from a health perspective you of course want to minimize contact with these kinds of substances.

IS IT ALWAYS BEST TO BOYCOTT PLASTICS?

There isn't a straight answer. Should you, for example, carry your shopping home in a plastic bag or in a fabric tote bag that you've brought yourself? If the plastic bag is used several times and is then recycled the right way or incinerated, it can be a better alternative to a fabric bag made from conventionally produced cotton, since that is incredibly bad for the environment. Read more on page 63.

WHERE DO YOU START?

The kitchen is where it's most important to go on a plastic diet. Why? Because the problem is mainly about plastic releasing toxins into our food, which will then go straight into the body. These harmful substances leach out at a higher rate when the plastic is heated. So that's where we should start – get rid of all plastic that comes into contact with food and heat.

START WITH WHAT YOU'VE ALREADY GOT

It can be expensive to replace your utensils, but if you are someone who saves food packaging such as ice-cream containers or margarine tubs, that's a perfect place to start.

Get rid of all those thriftily saved plastic ice-cream tubs. They are not made to withstand heat and so can, if used in the wrong way, be one of the biggest culprits. Plastic containers that have been specifically produced to store food are labelled with a glass and fork symbol on the base. In this type of plastic, the added substances are more stable – they don't get released into the food as easily and should therefore be okay for our health. But they're not better for the environment. So let's save plastic usage for the areas where it really can't be replaced, such as heart pumps.

For leftover food, it's better to use those empty glass jars you have saved instead. But here comes the next culprit – watch out for the lids! The inside of the lid often has a coating that can release toxic substances, and the little soft vacuum seal on the inside edge can be made from PVC.

1. Use glass jars, but make sure that the food doesn't come into contact with the lid.
2. Use a small plate as a lid over a jar in the fridge. It's not as tight-fitting but will certainly work for a day or so.

THE PLASTIC DIET TO-DO LIST

Cooking
TEFLON-COATED FRYING PAN – swap for cast iron.
FRYING UTENSILS – swap for stainless steel (can be used in cast-iron pans).
CHOPPING BOARD – swap for wood (oak is naturally antibacterial – oil it from time to time with standard cooking oil). Use a chopping board made from glass or porcelain for meat, chicken and fish.
KETTLE – swap for a steel one.

Washing-up
WASHING-UP BRUSH – swap for a wooden one.
DISH-CLOTH – it's best to use one made from linen (has bacteria-resistant qualities, can be easily washed in the washing machine and will last 5 to 10 years).

Storage
PLASTIC CONTAINERS – start with getting rid of those not intended for hot food.
CLING FILM – swap for a cheese dome or beeswax wraps.
FREEZER BAGS – bread can be frozen wrapped in a linen towel for a few days; some items, such as vegetables, can be frozen without packaging.
BOWLS, JUGS – swap for stainless steel, porcelain or glass.

Baking
BAKING PAPER – grease the tin instead or use recycled, compostable paper.
BAKING TINS with non-stick coating – swap for porcelain or glass.

Drinks
PET BOTTLES – don't reuse as water bottles, use bottles made from glass or steel for your workout.
STRAWS – swap for paper straws.

THE RIGHT WASTE IN THE RIGHT PLACE

Every year in the UK, we each throw away approximately 400 kilos of waste per person. Of the 26 million tonnes of waste produced annually in the UK, 12 million tonnes are recycled, and 14 million tonnes are sent to landfill sites. That includes fully usable garments; please consider donating your clothes, don't throw them away.

But it's not just textiles that we need to last longer, it goes for everything we consume. Use what you've got for much longer, and then recycle by sorting your waste correctly!

WASTE SORTING

Waste sorting saves energy and natural resources. Here are a few concrete examples of what we can gain:

- 1 kilo recycled plastics = 2 kilos reduction in carbon dioxide emissions
- 1 recycled tin = the energy equivalent of watching TV for 7 hours
- 1 recycled newspaper = 38 cups of coffee
- 1 bag recycled food waste = enough biogas to drive a car 2.5 kilometres (1½ miles)
- 1 tonne recycled paper = 14 trees

RECYCLING

ALUMINIUM can be recycled an unlimited number of times and gives an energy saving of 95 per cent in comparison to producing a new one from scratch. Can be turned into a new can, a road sign or blinds.

NEWSPAPER can be recycled 5–7 times and will save approximately 65 per cent energy in comparison to producing a new one from scratch. Gets turned into newspapers and toilet paper.

GLASS can be reused an unlimited number of times. Reusing glass reduces carbon emissions by 41 per cent and saves 20 per cent energy.

PLASTIC can be recycled, but not for the same thing, since the quality of plastic will reduce at each stage. PET bottles are made from one of the stronger plastics and can be used to make polyester fleece, but it doesn't work in reverse. Hard plastics can be turned into plant pots; soft plastics can be turned into bags, sacks or furniture.

CLEVER WASTE-SORTING TIPS

The more we sort our waste, the more space it will take up in our homes. How do you manage it? The most efficient way is to sort it straightaway and to make it as easy as possible so that you actually do it. It doesn't hurt if the solution is also aesthetically pleasing. Here are a few ideas:

IF SPACE IS LIMITED, get a bench or an old kitchen sofa with storage space and you will benefit from a dual function. As a bonus, you'll gain practical seating space in the hallway or at the dining table. Here you can store paper, newspaper and cardboard.

FOR SORTING messier waste, you will have to divide up the sofa's storage space with several plastic compartments.

USE A HANGING SHOE ORGANIZER with multiple compartments, preferably one that can be closed. Hang it in the hallway and store what is destined for recycling there. It's simple to take down and carry to the recycling centre by bicycle.

USE CABINETS WITH TILTING DOORS (intended for shoes). They can be useful in the hallway, kitchen and other areas in the house.

IF YOU HAVE A GARDEN, the plastic benches meant for storing the seat cushions of your outdoor furniture could be turned into a recycling station. There you can sort, for example, newspapers, carboard, plastics and bottles. It's the same principle as the kitchen sofa, but you can keep the benches outside and they will be easier to keep clean.

PLASTIC AND FLEECE

Did you know that a fleece jacket or blanket sheds thousands of microplastic particles every time it's washed? They are so tiny that our sewage plants can't catch them, which means that millions of microplastic particles end up in our waterways every hour. It's easy to understand the problem with plastic bags in the ocean when you see pictures of turtles and seals that have got tangled. But this microscopic plastic is just as damaging for smaller animals and organisms, such as mussels, starfish and worms. Two out of three blue mussels examined on the west coast of Sweden had ingested plastic particles that can contain harmful substances, such as flame retardants and plasticizers. Plastic in small organisms means that larger animals that eat them ingest the plastic in turn, and eventually it will end up in the food on our own plates.

Until very recently 40 per cent of all plastic was made into single-use items such as cutlery, straws, balloon sticks and cotton buds. Since 2021, these are all banned in the EU. But it's a good idea to also give up those single-use objects that are still allowed. Here's how to do it:

• Get a reusable cup if you often buy takeaway coffee.
• Buy a water bottle made of glass or metal.
• Minimize the use of plastic bags.

Over 300 million tonnes of plastic are produced every year. A negligible amount of this is biodegradable or made from renewable sources. Between 5 and 13 million tonnes of plastic end up in the ocean every year. There is a chance that there will be more plastic than fish in our seas by 2050.

The Wettex cleaning cloth is a Swedish invention from the 1940s, and widely available internationally. The name Wettex comes from 'wet textile'. The material is cellulose and cotton, which is biodegradable. It will decompose in the compost after six to eight weeks. It can also be put in the recycling with corrugated cardboard.

WHEN YOU FEEL INSPIRED
A few ideas to make changes
without buying new:

We've talked a lot about practical matters, but what about comfort? What about when you want to ring the changes at home?

GATHER ALL kitchen utensils in a nice jar – it will become a beautiful decoration.

LEAN CHOPPING BOARDS against the wall and use them as an eye-catching feature.

PROP A LARGE SILVER TRAY against the wall to use as a noticeboard.

USE A BAKING TRAY as a splashback behind the cooker.

LOOK FOR CROCHETED POTHOLDERS at a flea market, if you don't have any already. They are often thick, good quality and well made. They are pretty just as they are, so leave them out. But there are also fun projects you can make with old potholders, such as joining them together to make bunting, or sewing several together for a cushion cover or a little blanket.

USE EGG CUPS as vases for small flowers.

PAINT the kitchen cupboards with eco-friendly paint.

USE WALLPAPER OR PAINT to make an accent wall; just a small area can be enough to catch the eye.

PAINT A CUPBOARD DOOR or section of wall with blackboard paint and use as a planner board.

LOOK FOR NEW doorknobs at a flea market.

THE BEDROOM

a place for dreams

FOR ME, the image of a restful bedroom
is a cool room with a bed made up with
freshly washed sheets that have been
hung outside to dry in the warm summer
breeze. A simple flower in a small glass,
a stearin candle and a good book on the
bedside table. It would preferably be quiet
as well, with just some birdsong drifting
through the window.

And what about the environmental point
of view? What is the most sustainable
way of sleeping? Here are a few thoughts.

ECO-BOOST THE BEDROOM
Seven clever tips

LOWER THE TEMPERATURE: Having the radiator
in the bedroom set at a degree lower than you are
used to is a good way to save energy and care for the
environment. It's a good idea generally to lower the
overall temperature in the house. When you go away,
it's enough to keep it at 15°C indoors.

VENTILATE: To get cool and fresh air to sleep in,
while at the same time ventilating sustainably, it's
best to open a window wide, preferably with a cross-
breeze coming through, for 10 minutes. But avoid
keeping the window ajar for hours on end. Why?
By ventilating quickly, the air will get exchanged
without the furniture, floor and walls cooling down,
so you don't have to turn up the heating to get the
warmth back.

CURTAINS: Lower the blinds and pull the curtains
shut at dusk so that less of the warm air inside the
home can get out.

POTTED PLANTS: Sit a pot plant on the windowsill.
Why? Green plants are good for indoor air quality,
and some are particularly good to keep in the
bedroom. Read more about potted plants on page 76.

THE BED: If possible, buy an eco-certified bed. Read
more about beds on page 61.

SHEETS: Old is best. Why? Read more about textiles
on page 62.

WASH LESS: Shake duvets and blankets and hang
them out to air from time to time instead of washing
them. Why? Not washing when it isn't necessary
saves energy. Read more about laundry on page 72.

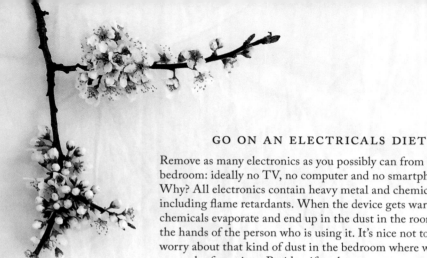

GO ON AN ELECTRICALS DIET

Remove as many electronics as you possibly can from the bedroom: ideally no TV, no computer and no smartphone. Why? All electronics contain heavy metal and chemicals, including flame retardants. When the device gets warm, the chemicals evaporate and end up in the dust in the room and on the hands of the person who is using it. It's nice not to have to worry about that kind of dust in the bedroom where we spend so much of our time. Besides, if we have a computer or TV in the bedroom, the room will be associated with something that raises the pulse instead of promoting rest. It's better to help the brain wind down by avoiding blue light from a screen before you go to bed.

EASY TO CLEAN

A significant amount of the chemical particles we want to avoid is gathered in dust. Anywhere that has a lot of textiles, like the bedroom, automatically generates a lot of dust. So we have every reason to keep this room in particular clean. (Read more about eco-friendly cleaning on page 132.)

An easily cleaned bedroom has:

• As little stuff as possible.

• Furniture that is easy to move.

• A wall-mounted bedside shelf – bedside tables will easily gather dust and make the area around the bed seem crowded.

• Good storage for clothes, such as hooks on the wall or a free-standing coat rack.

• No carpets or rugs.

MULTIPLE FUNCTIONS

If you live in a small space, which is best from an environmental perspective, one room may need to have multiple functions. You'll have to think creatively. This is how we worked it out.

The layout of our house and how we use the rooms has varied over the years that we've lived there. No room has ever had an obvious function. All the rooms are about the same size, apart from the kitchen, which is tiny. Everything is a bit undecided, which can seem impractical. And it is, but I choose to look at it as charming, and it invites us to make our own choices.

When the kids were little my husband and I slept in the living room. As it was right next to what would become the kids' bedroom and play area, it had a lot of advantages: think running between rooms and swapping beds in the night when you're so tired that you can't even remember how you ended up in there the next morning.

In the daytime, the double bed in the middle of the living room became a natural play area for the kids and their friends. It might not always have felt very hygienic, but in a way, it worked out pretty well; after a few hours of jumping and bouncing on the bed, it was well aired. At bedtime, all that was left to do was to shake off the sheets and open the window to air.

And that double bed has lasted really well. When we had our youngest son, quite a few years after the other children, we thought, well, now it's time for a new bed. But for various reasons, we never got round to it. What held me back, among other things, was the thought of all the chemicals that can come with newly produced beds, and which would likely have disappeared from the old one after several years of use.

You should, however, keep in mind that chemicals such as flame retardants in mattresses are there to make the furniture less flammable. The idea is for the retardant to last for the bed's whole lifetime, that is around twenty years.

NEW BED?
Eco-certification and cosy times

We spend a large part of our lives in bed – a third in fact.
Therefore, it's important to carefully think through the purchase
of a new bed, especially if you know there will be small children
nearby, as they are extra-sensitive to environmental toxins. If it's
economically possible, try to buy an eco-certified bed.

Otherwise, start by getting an eco-certified mattress topper.
That's a good step in the direction of having organic and
sustainable materials closest to your body. Look for organic
cotton, horsehair and different kinds of grain.

There is a range of different types of eco-certification, and
what you really have to watch out for is that the certification
applies to *all* the layers that make up the bed. The textile might
be eco-certified, but also check what the filling in the mattress
is made from.

The most important elements to avoid are flame retardants,
synthetic latex, foam materials and particle board, which can
all release toxic chemicals.

SHEETS — OLD IS BEST

When you have chosen the right bed it's time to think about the rest of the elements: duvets, pillows (make sure to check both filling and outer material) and sheets. Thoroughly laundered old cotton or linen sheets are the best that you can sleep between. Any possible chemical treatments will have been washed away, and they are therefore even better from an environmental perspective than organically produced new sheets. Just the fact that they are second hand is a gain in itself. If you still want to buy new, choose organic sheets that are responsibly produced.

If you like patterned sheets, make sure to choose durable patterns that are either woven into the fabric or printed through the fabric and not merely on top. Plastic prints often contain plasticizing phthalates that release hormone-disrupting substances. Read more about plastic on page 41.

If you feel a bit sceptical about buying used sheets, place them in the freezer for a week before you wash and use them. That way you can make sure that every single little mite is stone-cold dead!

ON COTTON

• Of all the world's textiles that are produced today, 40 per cent are made from cotton fibres.

• Cotton is often cultivated in dry areas and will then need to be irrigated, making it one of the most water-intensive crops in the world.

• To produce 1 kilo of cotton from seedling to finished fabric requires 29,000 litres of water.

• Cotton takes up only 2.5 per cent of the world's plantations in area, but uses 25 per cent of the total amount of insecticides and 11 per cent of all herbicides.

• Organic cotton is cultivated without toxins.

• Organically cultivated cotton lasts up to three times as long as traditionally cultivated cotton, as the fibres haven't been affected by chemicals.

• Less than 1 per cent of all cotton produced is organic.

ON FLAX (LINEN) AND HEMP

Flax (linen) and hemp are textile fibres that can grow in nutrition-poor soil and survive a cooler, wetter climate. Their cultivation therefore needs less irrigation, chemical fertilizers and pesticides than cotton. A textile made from flax or hemp is both more durable and more dirt-repellent than, say, cotton.

Advantages of linen sheets:

• Can withstand dirt better than cotton and therefore don't have to be washed as frequently.

• Cool when it's warm and warm when it's cold.

• Unbleached linen sheets = less environmental stress.

That said, since it takes a lot of energy to extract the fibres from flax and hemp and turn them into textiles, the effect on the climate can end up at least as high as for cotton. It's a tricky equation.

The softer and smoother the linen sheets are, the better quality. This is easy to check just by feeling them with your hand.

ON WOOL

Wool has a lot of good qualities:

• Easy to find locally produced, organic and untreated.

• Naturally heat regulating.

• Naturally flame-resistant qualities.

• Dirt repellent – it's often enough to air it (preferably when the weather is damp) instead of washing it.

'Sleep away from all damned quarrels
Flee from the well of sorrows
Wake up with a summer soul
And a rose in your mouth.'

Greta Digman, loosely quoting
Elisabet Hermodsson

WHEN YOU FEEL INSPIRED
A few ideas to make changes
without buying new:

• Use an old door as a headboard.

• Use a tablecloth as a bedspread, or as a curtain.

• Hang up a kimono, a nightgown or a pretty blouse on the wall as decoration.

• Use a stool, a pile of books or an upside-down basket as a bedside table.

• Swap lamps with those from another room.

Coco Chanel JUSTINE PICARDIE

the stylists guide to

Style Diaries PRESTEL

A GOOD NIGHT'S SLEEP
Eight tips – classics that are worth repeating
and a few new ones

• Keep the bedroom cool, between 16 and 19°C.

• Keep the light out by using dark curtains.

• No coffee later than six hours before bedtime.

• Turn the clock away from you so you don't look at it through the night.

• Write down any worries before you go to bed and leave them there until the next day.

• Wake up at the same time every morning, even at weekends if possible.

• Avoid screens for at least 30 minutes before you go to bed. Blue light from a TV, computer or smartphone suppresses the brain's own sleep hormone.

• Fresh air and daylight help the circadian rhythm, so try to spend some time outside every day.

THE WARDROBE

A flowery dress, a few T-shirts and an embroidered blouse.
A velvet jacket that I just couldn't resist stroking with my hand,
and an owl-print jumper. This is what I found in the kitchen. In
the living room, in piles hanging over the banister and in every
bed on the first floor were more piles of clothes. The coffee was
brewing, the cakes were served, everything was there – it was
time for a clothes swap day at my friend's house.

This ingenious idea is becoming more and more popular. You can
find local clothes swap parties online, or arrange one yourself.

REUSING

Why is it so important to find good ways to reuse clothes?
Because 80 per cent of a garment's total environmental impact
is created at the production stage. The clothing industry
emits more greenhouse gases than the aviation and shipping
industries combined. For example, approximately 10,000
litres of water and 1 kilo of chemicals are required to produce
a single kilo of cotton. And did you know that the UK is the
fourth largest producer of textile waste in Europe? Each Briton
throws away about 3 kilos of textiles every year. Seven out of
ten people shop for clothes every month or more often, and the
same number only wear half of the clothes they own.

Apart from it being incredibly wasteful to throw away
wearable clothes, it's difficult to recycle textiles. Extracting
fibres from textiles to sew new clothes is very difficult. Over
half of all textile waste in the UK ends up in landfill.

Buy fewer clothes and better quality, preferably second hand.
Take good care of your clothes and they will last for longer.
Last but not least: mend clothes that have got damaged.

ECO-BOOST THE LAUNDRY

Looking after our clothes properly, so they can be used over a long period of time and hopefully by many people, is a good deed for the environment. How do you go about it? The most important thing is to wash them correctly, since washing will wear down both the clothes and the environment through energy consumption and emissions. Laundry is a big part of a garment's total energy cost. In one study, people's laundry baskets were examined and it turned out that only 7 per cent of the contents was properly dirty. So it's a good idea to wear your clothes for longer in between washes. Sometimes it's enough just to air them.

When it's eventually time to put on a wash, always only do a full load and use the right dosage of detergent (not too much). Use the lowest temperature you can. Washing at 40°C instead of 60°C will bring large gains in energy consumption.

Fabric softener contains a range of chemicals that are released with the wastewater, and it isn't actually necessary. If you want your clothes to feel a bit softer, you can add a dash of distilled vinegar instead. And if you want a nicer fragrance than the laundry detergent provides, try mixing your own eco-friendly fabric softener.

HOMEMADE ECO-FRIENDLY FABRIC SOFTENER

200 ml distilled vinegar (24%)
500 ml water
7 drops lavender essential oil
Mix together and store in a glass bottle. Shake before use and add two tablespoons in the fabric softener compartment. This will also keep your washing machine cleaner and fresher.

FOUR FIT CHALLENGE

Have you heard of the Four Fit Challenge? It's an initiative that aims to use just four garments in different combinations for one week. This challenge can be helpful to try and get used to the idea that you don't have to change into new clothes every day. You can actually wear the exact same outfit two days in a row without any problem.

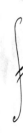

Avoid tumble dryers, which both wear out the clothes and use a lot of energy. The worst energy culprit of all is a large electric 'drying cabinet'. Let your clothes air-dry on a washing line (outside if possible), clothes horse or drying rack.

HANG IT UP

Hang up clothes that have been worn but are not ready to be washed in a separate place instead of just throwing everything in a pile or the laundry basket.

It's best to have three stations:
• Completely clean – the wardrobe
• Semi-clean – hanger
• Not clean at all – laundry basket

When I was little my parents had a coat stand in their bedroom. There they would hang belts and shirts, dressing gowns and jeans in a big jumble. The only problem was probably that the garments that were furthest towards the centre would hang there for such a long time that they were forgotten about. One clever tip is to fit peg rails along one wall in the bedroom. Just hang up your jeans using the belt loops and shirts by the collar.

WHEN YOU FEEL INSPIRED
A few ideas to make changes
without buying new:

• Sort and organize. You will get a better overview of what you've got. Perhaps you will find something you've forgotten about, or that can be combined in a new way.

• If you are tired of a garment, perhaps you can remake it. Anyone can cut the legs off an old pair of jeans.

• Check if a garment that has been torn can be mended. Decide to invest some time doing that, or take it to a tailor. Unfortunately, it can cost as much to mend something as it does to buy a new item, so you have to remember the environmental aspect. But if it's a favourite garment, you will wear it again.

• Garments that you know you will never wear again could be turned into something completely new; for example, a blouse, a jumper or a scarf can become a cushion cover.

HOUSE PLANTS

make the air cleaner

ANYONE VISITING THE HOME of friends of mine is greeted in the stairwell by enormous weeping fig plants that stretch themselves towards the sunlight from various directions. Weeping fig works particularly well on staircases as it doesn't require much light. Through the weathered door you're welcomed by a curtain of greenery, made up of plants that hang from the ceiling. And behind a veil of spider plants and devil's ivy further in, you catch a glimpse of two computers and a home office. The idea was to create the feeling of a garden indoors, with the plants also contributing to creating fresher air in the home. A win-win situation all round.

CLEAN AIR

How do we know that potted plants contribute to better air quality indoors? And how does it work? Research started in the 1980s in conjunction with plans for a manned base on the moon. The air inside a spaceship was a big problem, since all technical equipment emitted chemical substances that were bad to inhale. Therefore, they wanted to create a micro ecosystem inside the space base and purify the air that way. It turned out to work well. Just as the forest purifies our air outside, plants could purify the air inside, especially in a closed system room, but also in a standard home.

Toxins that are particularly well absorbed by plants include:
- BENZENE: Found in solvents, cleaning products, plaster, wallpaper, ceiling panels, textiles, paint and rubber.
- FORMALDEHYDE: Found in particle board, plaster, furniture, wallpaper, textiles, paper products and paint.
- TRICHLOROETHYLENE: Found in cleaning products, glue and varnish.

Scientific studies have shown that plants can have a positive effect on the air quality in our homes, with NASA scientists recommending at least two good-sized plants for every 9 square metres (100 square feet) of indoor space. The more leaves you have, the more toxins can be removed from your living space!

OXYGEN

Another important quality of plants is photosynthesis, through which they absorb carbon dioxide and release oxygen, contributing to fresher air. At night, when photosynthesis pauses, the reverse happens, meaning that the plant absorbs oxygen and releases carbon dioxide, just like humans. Certain plants, however, particularly those that are native to deserts, actively absorb carbon dioxide from the air at night to store in their leaves. This means that the stomata (plant pores) aren't opened in the day when it's hot, but instead at night, when it's cool. This way, less liquid evaporates. These kinds of plants, such as aloe vera, are therefore the ones that you want in the bedroom.

Potted plants have the ability to effectively raise the humidity levels in a room. Around 90 per cent of the water that you give it will evaporate with increased humidity as a result.

THE BEST PLANTS

Which plants are best for the environment then? Well, it depends a little on how you look at it and which features should be considered. The spider plant will end up high on the list if you consider characteristics such as how easy it is to look after, how hardy it is and how easy to propagate. It's not, however, the best when it comes to absorbing toxins. But it's better to have a living plant with reasonable absorption than no plant at all or, even worse, a bunch of dead brown ferns in a corner. The sword fern is often named as one of the best plants for absorbing toxins, but it's also fairly difficult to care for.

Most palm plants are good humidifiers, while ivy is the plant that absorbs the most kinds of toxins, although not the highest amount of every toxin. Really good plants, all things considered, are often the old favourites:

• Spider plant

• Devil's ivy

• Snake plant

• Peace lily

• Ivy

• Palm

• Jade plant

• Weeping fig

• Aloe vera

ON WATERING

To know how to water different types of potted plants, a simple trick is to look at the leaves.

• SUCCULENTS need less water since they can store it in their thick leaves.

• PLANTS WITH THIN and tender leaves often need more water.

• FLOWERING PLANTS that are in bloom need more care and water.

• GREEN PLANTS without flowers generally need less water.

My grandmother always left a full watering can out to let the water aerate ahead of the next watering, which is good for the plants.

How often should you water a standard sized pot?

• Standard watering means 100 ml per week and is suitable for ivies and peace lilies, for example.

• Moderate watering means 150 ml every second or third week and applies to, among others, devil's ivy, snake plants and wax plants.

• Generous watering means a thorough watering two to three times a week. Spider plants, azaleas, hibiscus and hydrangeas and other plants like this. But keep in mind that more plants die from too much water than from too little.

CUTTINGS

A good deed for the environment is to not buy new plants every year, but instead propagate them. Take cuttings and give them away, perhaps instead of a bouquet?

How to take cuttings:

• A cutting should be approximately 5 centimetres (2 inches) long. Cut it off right below a pair of leaves, as this is where the new roots can then grow out.

• Remove the lowest leaves so that you get a small stem.

• Place one or two cuttings in a glass or glass jar and watch how the roots develop beautifully.

• Wait for a couple of weeks until the roots have grown a bit and then plant in a small pot.

• If you want, you can plant the fresh cutting in sowing compost straightaway, and the new roots will grow straight into the soil.

• Water it, but not too much or the roots will run the risk of rotting.

• Leave the pot in a light place but not in direct sunlight.

• Turn the pot occasionally to make sure all sides get exposed to the light.

FOR A LITTLE MORE FINESSE, did you know that several of our most common potted plants don't need any soil? They will thrive in just water. This is called hydroponics and works well with plants such as painter's palette and common ivy. A geranium cutting will also last for a long time in water. Use a vase or jar, or even a bottle. Remove the soil from the plant, wash the roots clean and place in room-temperature water, just enough to cover the roots. Change the water occasionally.

THE LIVING ROOM

hang out on an eco-sofa

CRYSTAL CHANDELIER
or slide?

This was the title of a Swedish radio programme (Kristallkrona eller rutschkana?) hosted by the interior designer Lena Larsson in the 1940s. It looked at the untouched reception room that few people used, while new homes didn't have enough space for children to play.

At our place we go for both. Perhaps not exactly a crystal chandelier, but at least my grandparents' nice lamp, fit for the salons, and a slide that my dad built for me and my brother when we were little. Both are perfect in the living room.

And the living room is exactly what it sounds like – a room that is lived in every day. Even if you like to hang out in the kitchen/diner, not just to cook but also to do homework and chat about what's happened during the day, it's the living room sofa that you long for after a hard day.

ECO-BOOST THE LIVING ROOM

Eco problems can be found in every room. In the living room, culprit number one is the sofa. It's just as important to look at the labelling here as when you buy a bed. Is the sofa eco-certified? What exactly is certified, if so? The wooden frame? The textile? The filling?

Most sofas and other upholstered furniture are treated with flame retardants to lower the fire risk. It's mainly the plastic foam in the furniture that can emit chemicals, including chlorinated phosphorous flame retardant. If the frame is made from particle board it can also release formaldehyde.

That doesn't sound too good. But research into these particular chemicals is ongoing, with new findings published all the time. So although it's important to be aware of the problems with flame retardants, you probably don't have to throw out your sofa immediately. Besides, the absolute largest exposure to brominated flame retardants that we get probably doesn't come from contact with furniture or dust, but actually through our food, such as oily fish. This is due to chemical contamination that the sewage plans can't catch and which therefore ends up in our waterways. Read more on page 48.

GOOD WOOD — FSC

One of the factors contributing to the earth's rising temperature is deforestation. One-fifth of this covers areas harvested for timber that goes towards, among other things, the production of furniture and other items that use wood as a raw material. It's therefore important to check that wooden furniture is made from wood from forests that are managed in a responsible way. Forest Stewardship Council (FSC) is an independent international organization with this aim in mind. They give a certification according to environmental, social and economic criteria.

*Turn to page 139 for expert tips on
buying second-hand furniture.*

The best sofa is second hand, well used and well aired.

NEW SOFA?
Some sustainable options

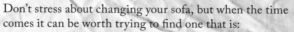

Don't stress about changing your sofa, but when the time comes it can be worth trying to find one that is:

• Filled with natural materials, such as wool or horsehair, not with foam rubber, plastic foam or similar.

• Without any filling at all – a daybed made from solid wood and untreated textiles to which you can add cushions yourself.

• Second hand, well used and aired. It's best if it dates from the time before large amounts of chemicals were introduced. Above all, avoid furniture from the 1970s, '80s and '90s. Several kinds of flame retardants were used then that are banned today.

To be on the safe side, I'd recommend choosing a sofa that was made before 1950. Since the 1950s, the global production of chemicals has increased from 7 to 400 million tonnes per year, according to the EU.

WHAT FILLING MATERIAL HAS BEEN USED?

During the 1950s and '60s furniture production was rationalized and materials such as foam rubber and latex were developed. These were incredibly easy to use and upholstering was done in a flash, but it wasn't anticipated that sunlight would break down these materials to make them harden, crumble and smell bad. Since 1980 a filling made from polyether – oil-based, highly resilient cold foam – is often used instead.

Some chairs preserved from the eighteenth century are filled with straw, common haircap moss and horsehair, and covered with woven linen. All durable materials that have lasted to this day, 300 years on. Of course, there is the odd feature that you might not have a full overview of – paint, varnish and so on – but hopefully they should have been rubbed off by now anyway.

MY SECOND-HAND SOFAS

Around the same time as we moved into our house it was time to replace the sofa that my husband had (genuinely) found in a skip. For the first (and maybe also the last) time we bought a brand-new sofa and I thought it smelled bad straightaway. Smell is one of the main factors you should particularly be aware of when identifying chemical treatments as a lay person. If something smells a bit synthetic and unpleasant, it's likely because it contains something more or less toxic, like flame retardant for example.

Today we have two real second-hand bargains, Chippendale sofas from the 1930s that have been done up a little. One came from an online auction site, the other from a second-hand shop, and both were just as cheap. What I really like about them is their airiness – that there is so much wood and that the rattan lets the air flow through in the best kind of way. The drawback is that this kind of sofa often has floppy cushions that slide around. We solved this by reusing the cushions from our old sofa. (Yes, that's right, from the bad-smelling sofa… as it turned out, it was the frame itself and not the cushions that smelled.) With a bit of force, they just fit in snugly against each other and become a perfect and steady seating surface.

I usually cover the cushions with sheepskins from the time my aunt realized her life's dream. With her husband, she bought a farm with both sheep and horses and turned the barn into a bed and breakfast. They arrived in cherry blossom season and, of course, named the place Cherry Farm. Well, I digress, but it means I know for certain that our sheepskins aren't treated with any kind of chemicals.

The spring mattress from the children's old cot, which I sewed a new cover for in blue velvet, became the cushion for the other sofa. It might not be a super-durable fabric for furniture, but it means it's not treated with flame retardant either. Besides, it's easy to remove and wash and to replace when it is worn out or if I get tired of it. That said, next time I will remember to use linen, which is both more durable and naturally dirt-resistant (see page 64).

WHEN YOU FEEL INSPIRED
A few ideas to make changes
without buying new:

REMOVE THINGS

Sometimes removing stuff can have a bigger effect than adding stuff. Try it! Remove all small objects. Then put back only the things you like most. Perhaps it's a chair that should be removed? Or that little table that is nice, but is usually in the way.

OBJECTS

• Move small items around.

• Gather them into one spot rather than leaving them spread out all over the place.

• Rethink and create completely new still lifes from what you've got at home.

ART

• Rehang your wall art.

• Gather everything into one space.

• Or do the opposite: remove everything and let one piece of art sing.

• Try to mix something else in with the wall art – a sculpture, a mirror, an empty frame.

• Don't forget children's drawings.

• Hang plates up on the wall.

• If you have a straight line above your gallery wall, perhaps try the straight line at the bottom instead? Or no straight line at all, just hang them at random.

• Hang your art asymmetrically, keeping one striking piece to one side, for example, or use the rule of thirds by hanging art across one-third of the sofa.

A friend suggested the idea of first hanging all your paintings properly, with well thought-through measurements, then taking everything down again and hanging the art at random on the hooks that are now up. I think it still requires a certain level of aesthetics to make it work of course, but doesn't it sound a bit crazy and fun?

REARRANGING THE FURNITURE

• Move furniture away from the wall – 10 centimetres (4 inches) is enough. This will give a sense of space, good flow through the room and the furniture won't block the radiators from spreading heat.

• Change the location of a large item such as the sofa or a bookshelf.

• Empty the whole room and rethink. Only put back what you really like and use.

• Try to bring in some of your garden furniture, if you have any. A garden chair can become a perfect place for a potted plant that needs raising a bit.

• If you have a desk left over, use it as a sideboard.

• Try putting the dining table somewhere new, or relocate your desk.

• If you're tired of your sofa, simply try draping it in fabric. A sheet can be enough, but a bedspread will work even better, as it gives a bit more stability.

FOLLOW THE SEASONS

• Summer: Remove the rugs and the curtains – it will bring light, air and energy to the room.

• Winter: Put the rugs down again and hang up the curtains for a snug, soft atmosphere.

• Try placing several rugs together to create a larger soft area. With rag rugs, you can even stitch them together to prevent them from sliding apart.

• Remove blankets and sheepskins in the summer, if you don't use them to cover something.

LIGHTING

lamps and candles

LED AND INCANDESCENT LIGHT BULBS

Lighting accounts for a quarter of household electricity use in an average home. It's therefore important to consider which type of light you use.

Nowadays it's unlawful to produce traditional incandescent light bulbs anywhere in the EU and UK. This is a good thing as the technology has not changed much since the light bulb was invented in 1879, with a lot of the energy being turned into heat instead of light. The LED bulb is the replacement that has proven to be most effective and give a comfortable light. An LED bulb uses 85 per cent less energy than an incandescent light bulb and lasts 25 times longer, a significant improvement.

In the era of the incandescent light bulb you would calculate the wattage, which measures effect, that is energy consumption, when choosing how bright a light should be. These days we calculate lumen instead, luminous flux. For a luminous flux of 300–500 lumen, you would need 40 watts for an old-fashioned light bulb, and only 3–5 watts for an LED bulb.

Electricity consumption in the EU is predicted to reduce by 39 billion kilowatt hours per year once all lights have been replaced with LED.

HOW LONG DOES 1 KILOWATT HOUR LAST?

Depending on what effect the appliance has, the length of time 1 kilowatt hour lasts varies:
- Gas hob burner (1,500 watt): 40 minutes
- Microwave oven (1,500 watt): 40 minutes
- Kettle (1,500 watt): 40 minutes
- Vacuum cleaner (1,400 watt): 43 minutes
- Filter coffee machine (800 watt): 1 hour and 15 minutes
- Incandescent light bulb (40 watt): 25 hours
- Low-energy light bulb (9 watt): 111 hours
- Mobile phone charger (5 watt): 200 hours

Household electricity: one-quarter goes on lighting, one-quarter on the fridge and freezer, one-quarter on home electronics and the remaining quarter on laundry, washing-up and cooking.

WHAT MAKES LIGHTING COMFORTABLE?

How we experience light is down to, among other things, the light's colour temperature and its colour rendering index. A low temperature will give a warm light with a large proportion of red tones, while a higher colour temperature will give a colder, more bluish light.

Different colour temperatures are suited to different things. A cold-toned light will give better contrast and is therefore good in a reading lamp, for example. If you want the same type of shine as a traditional incandescent light bulb, the colour temperature should range between 2,700 and 3,000 K.

Colour temperature is measured in Kelvins (K).
Colour rendering index is measured in Rendering average (Ra).

LIGHT SOURCES

As a rule, multiple light sources in a room will create a more comfortable environment, particularly during winter. It is a good idea to think seasonally here. How much natural light does the room get? The more daylight you let into your home, the less you'll need light from lamps, which means less energy consumption. Remember not to switch lights on merely from habit and to switch the lights off when you are leaving a room. Even with energy-smart lighting, it always pays to switch a light off when you don't need it.

HOW MANY LIGHTS?

On an average day, you will need between five and seven light sources in a room to make it feel comfortable. On the whole, it's more important to have accent lighting dotted around different areas of the room than to have one large lamp on the ceiling.

AMBIENT OR GENERAL LIGHTING: this can be a ceiling lamp, but also daylight from a window.

TASK LIGHTING: for example, floor or wall lamps or a reading lamp by a chair or sofa.

ACCENT LIGHTING: by a bookshelf or gallery wall, for example.

DECORATIVE LIGHTING: such as fairy lights or small lamps on a windowsill, sideboard or chest of drawers.

CANDLE LIGHTING: don't forget this – it's the best way to create a cosy ambience.

THE HEIGHT OF A LAMP

When hanging a lamp over a dining table, the most important thing is that the light is comfortable and you don't get blinded by it, which means avoiding hanging it so high that the bulb becomes irritating. You will also need to make sure that it doesn't hang too low and block the view of the person sitting opposite. The solution to this equation is that a good height is around 55 centimetres (21⅝ inches) from the top of the dining table.

CANDLES

The majority of candles are made from paraffin, which involves significant carbon dioxide emissions, and most also contain palm oil. Stearin, on the other hand, comes from animal or vegetable fats and is a cleaner and better choice. White stearin candles are the best since the colorants used in candles contain both metals and other chemicals. Vegan soy wax and beeswax candles are good options, too. The absolute best are Nordic Swan-labelled candles, which fulfil a number of strict requirements when it comes to soot, heavy metals, colorants and fragrances.

Look for tea lights without hard-to-recycle metal cups. You can buy
tea lights with plastic-free, compostable cups instead.

WHEN YOU FEEL INSPIRED
Make a nice candle-holder

Find something fun at a flea market and make
a candle-holder from a brick!

You will need:
• bolt
• brick
• stearin candle
• figurine

Method:
Secure the bolt to the brick with melted stearin
from the candle – press the bolt into position
and leave to set. Do the same with the figurine.
Then place the candle into the bolt and your
new candle-holder is ready!

FLOWERS
Non-toxic and climate smart

The Friday bouquet – a perfect way
to finish the week! Of course, it's
nice to treat yourself to flowers over
the weekend, but have you given
any thought to where the flowers
come from? For an environmentally
sustainable bouquet, it's important
to choose flowers that are produced
as locally as possible. Avoiding
transportation is a big environmental
gain. Climate-smart, locally grown
flowers are easiest to find when they
are in their natural blooming season.
Try and follow the seasons: early
tulips from March, lily of the valley
in March and April, peonies from
April, dahlias in July and so on.

WILDFLOWERS

The best bouquets are often the ones that you put together from some sprigs from the garden. Oxeye daisies, grass stems and peonies, cherry blossom and the spring's first birch twigs. Or those slightly squished bouquets with stalks too short picked by little children. Wildflowers are, of course, among the most beautiful. If you pick them, make sure to do so where they grow densely, so that flowers remain for others to enjoy. Use scissors so that you don't accidentally pull up their roots, and keep in mind that some species are protected.

A good tip is to mix bought flowers with wild ones. Perhaps a base of simple tulips from the supermarket mixed with sprigs from nature or blossoming branches, if you have pruned the apple tree. A bunch of grass from the edge of a ditch along with three bought peonies will become a festive bouquet.

THINK LIKE A FLORIST

In old Dutch paintings you can see fantastic flower bouquets, combinations of French fringed tulips and all sorts of other things. A bouquet of a single type of flower is gorgeous, but with a few simple tricks you can put together a mixed bouquet.

HOW TO MAKE A PROFESSIONAL BOUQUET:

• Use different kinds of plants together. Mix flowers with grasses or herbs, for example.

• While mixing different colours can often look great, a safe bet is to keep to one shade and you won't go wrong.

• Remove most of the green leaves so that the flower can be seen.

• Make sure there is a variety of different heights in the bouquet.

• Work to the rule of three – an odd number is more pleasing to the eye than an even number of the same kind in a bouquet.

THE TOP FLOWERS

TULIP SEASON at its peak starts these days as early as December and runs until April. Trumpet-shaped, parrot fringed, striped, multi-coloured or double, there are an incredible 600 different varieties of tulip in the world. It's not surprising the tulip is one of our favourite cut flower varieties, since it's very hardy and will keep for a long time with proper care.

When buying cut flowers, always look for those cultivated locally (check the label) to cut down on transport-related emissions. Some tulips are even grown in the UK! If you're buying foreign-grown blooms, Fairtrade flowers are a good choice as environmental protection is built in to Fairtrade practices. If you're growing your own, search for organic bulbs. Most of the bulbs available have been treated with chemical pesticides.

TULIP TIPS

• Buy tulips that have already opened slightly to show their colour. If the buds are fully closed there is a chance they have been harvested too early and might never open.

• Trim the tulips straight, then place them in cold water immediately. When the stem is cut, the plant quickly forms a coating to heal the wound, kind of like a scab. Get the flowers into water before this coating has time to form again.

• Leave the wrapping on for a while so that the stems get a chance to soak up water and stretch. (Unless, like me, you think that tulips that are soft and flexible and sprawl out are just as beautiful.)

• Top up with fresh water every day.

• Tulips don't need any extra plant food, but ice cubes can be refreshing since they like their water to be as cold as possible.

ROSES are another big favourite. Millions are sold every February, most, of course, for Valentine's Day! When it comes to roses, the environment situation isn't great: a standard bouquet can contain up to 16 different pesticides. Many roses that are sold in Europe come from East Africa and South America. The working conditions of those involved with the flowers' production are dismal, due to the extensive use of pesticides among other issues. Therefore, only buy those that are Fairtrade certified. Or consider buying something grown locally instead!

ROSE TIPS

• Trim the stems using long, diagonal cuts. They need a cut surface area as big as possible to be able to soak up water more easily.

• Remove all leaves that are beneath the water surface. This will prevent bacteria growth in the water.

• Roses want warm water, as hot as possible from the tap.

If the roses are drooping:
• Wrap them in newspaper to reduce evaporation.

• Give them fresh diagonal cuts.

• Give them proper hot water.

• Place the wrapped flowers, in the hot water, in a cool place overnight.

HOMEMADE ECO-FRIENDLY PLANT FOOD

Instead of using chemical plant food – that plastic sachet that comes with your bouquet – it's easy to make your own organic plant food.

You will need:
1 litre water
2 tsp distilled vinegar (12%)
3–15 sugar cubes

Mix the ingredients together and stir until the sugar has dissolved. Pour into a bottle and put a cap on. The batch is enough for several bouquets: use approximately 100 ml for each.

The vinegar reduces the water's pH value, which limits bacteria growth and makes the bouquet last longer. The sugar gives the flowers nutrition and will help the buds to open. The harder the stem, the more sugar cubes you'll need.

Keep in mind that only flowers with hard stems need extra nutrition. Flowers with soft stems, such as tulips, can instead be given a teaspoon of potato starch or baking powder to keep them fresh for longer.

HEALTHY FLOWERS

Some cut flowers are proven to absorb toxic chemicals from the indoor air. Best of all are gerberas and chrysanthemums. Both can be found eco-certified, even though it's still rare. Gerberas originate from South Africa and are sensitive to cooler temperatures, while chrysanthemums can be planted in the garden in Northern Europe. Since chrysanthemums can thrive in our cooler climate it's also easier to find them grown in an eco-friendly way.

WHEN YOU FEEL INSPIRED
A few ideas to make changes without buying new:

• Use the odd glass as a vase.

• Place several bottles together and use them as vases.

• Use an old metal tin as a vase, but remember to place a glass jar inside so the water doesn't leak out.

• Arrange a few egg cups in a row on the table; this works just as well at both Easter and Christmas – fill with little spruce sprigs for the latter.

THE BATHROOM

your private spa

ECO-FRIENDLY BATHROOM DREAMS

New, fresh bathrooms are all well and good, but I immediately fell for this 1960s dream in turquoise-green tones. The wallpaper with motifs of full fruit bowls and flying pheasants. Tiles the same green as the Mediterranean Sea. A built-in bathtub with teak shelves above. Of course, it's always best not to rip existing interiors out of a house, not to swap old for newly produced materials, because of the energy impact the product will have on the environment. But when it comes to bathrooms in particular, there are certain factors and regulations to adhere to, so make sure you do your research before you decide what to do if an old-fashioned gem like this comes your way.

A tap with a constant slow drip will use around 1 litre of water per hour. In one day it will waste an amount of water equivalent to a whole shower fitted with a water-saving device. And in one year, the drips have become 9,000 litres of water, the equivalent of 60 full bathtubs!

BATH VS SHOWER

- It's best to shower quickly and efficiently instead of having a bath.
- A bath uses 150 litres of water and 5.6 kilowatt hours to heat the water.
- Showering for 5 minutes uses 60 litres of water and 2.2 kilowatt hours for heating.
- A short shower that lasts 5 instead of 15 minutes can reduce yearly consumption of hot water by 500 kilowatt hours.
- If you shorten the length of your shower by 2 minutes you will reduce greenhouse-gas emissions by 35 kilos per year.
- Replace your showerhead with a water-saving one. An old showerhead uses 12 litres of water per minute. A new water-saving one will only use half the amount of water.
- Change the washer when the tap starts leaking.

It's not that you should never take a bath again... but remember to enjoy it a bit more every time – see it as a spa moment.

MORE ECO-BOOSTING

- Switch off the electric towel rail when you're not using it. If it's left on all the time it can use 600 kilowatt hours per year.
- Use recycled and unbleached toilet tissue.
- Use the towels that you've got, for as long as you can. When it's time to change them, try to find organic and eco-certified terry cloth or linen towels.
- Swap a plastic shower curtain for a cotton-blend one. A thin lace curtain can also work as a divider.

THE BATHROOM CABINET – A BOOST FOR YOURSELF

Go through the bathroom cabinet and throw out anything that's old or expired. Consider whether you really need everything that's in there. A study has shown that the eight to twelve toiletries that on average we use every day (!) include between 85 and 168 different chemicals. Perhaps it's worth using less of something? That way you reduce the chemical impact and are kind to nature, the climate and your own body. Expired medicine should always be handed in at a pharmacy.

WHEN YOU FEEL INSPIRED
A few ideas to make changes
without buying new:

• Does your bathroom have a window? The humidity and the light will make it a perfect place for potted plants.

• If you don't have a window but still want greenery to soften up the bathroom you can put a branch of ivy in a glass – it will keep for quite a while without any daylight.

• If you have space, place loo rolls in a basket in the bathroom.

• Try to create a mirror wall from several old mirrors. The easiest way to do this is to fit a picture ledge along the wall to lean the mirrors on.

• Use a rag rug as a bathroom mat. It will give the room a completely different, softer atmosphere. Remove it if you know there will be a lot of water on the floor, but most rugs will dry well if you just hang them up.

• If you have space for a few decorative trinkets – a perfume bottle, a nice soap, a few pieces of jewellery – try to arrange them on a small tray to bring them together as a clear, fresh unit.

CLEANING

'Over walls and earth and trees and swinging sprays and tendrils the fair green veil
of tender little leaves had crept, and in the grass under the trees and the grey urns
in the alcoves and here and there everywhere, were touches or splashes of gold and
purple and white and the trees were showing pink and snow above... and there were
fluttering of wings and faint sweet pipes and humming and scents and scents.'

From *The Secret Garden* by Frances Hodgson Burnett

Ah, imagine the day that feels like this when it's time to spring clean!

NATURAL CLEANING

There is a long tradition of housewives' cleaning tips passed down through the generations and many clever tricks that don't require any chemicals. It's not necessary to use any chemical cleaning products at all.

Take green soap, for example, which is primarily made from pine oil and is suitable for everything: mopping the floors, cleaning the oven, removing stains, polishing jewellery, cleaning burnt pans, lubricating sticky locks, killing aphids… Together with some eco-friendly washing-up liquid, green soap is the only thing you need to keep your home clean. And water, of course.

EXTRA POWER

If you want some more power in your cleaning, two ingredients in the kitchen cupboard are particularly good for removing dirt in an eco-friendly way. One is bicarbonate of soda, which will remove stubborn dirt naturally. Baking powder works the same way, but the bicarbonate in it is mixed with other substances, so you need to use a larger amount to get the same effect. The other ingredient is distilled vinegar, which will kill bacteria and remove limescale.

THE BROOM
The cleaner's best friend

Mopping the floor to get rid of dust isn't very good for the environment. When the dirty water is emptied into the sink or toilet, it's flushed into the sewage plants. Unfortunately, they're not able to remove all the toxins there, as some particles are so tiny that they don't get caught by the filters and instead are flushed out into our groundwater, back into the water cycle and eventually through our kitchen taps again.

The best way to clean is instead to… sweep! Make sure to have a nice broom so that you want to keep it out – it's so much easier than having to drag out the vacuum cleaner. Discard what you have swept up in the general waste bin. You can reach that annoying bit of dust at the back of the sofa with a dust mop. By not using the vacuum cleaner you will save the equivalent amount of energy that 175 low-energy bulbs would use during their whole lifetime.

HOMEMADE CLEANING SOLUTIONS

FOR THE BATHROOM:
200 ml water
50 ml distilled vinegar (12%)
3–4 drops washing-up liquid
Dip a sponge into the mixture, rub over the surface to be cleaned
and then wipe with a cloth.

FOR THE TOILET:
Pour 50 ml bicarbonate of soda and a dash of distilled vinegar into
the toilet. Leave to work overnight. Scrub clean and flush out in
the morning.

FOR THE WASHING MACHINE:
If you always wash your laundry at a low temperature, which is good
for the environment, the washing machine can start to smell a little
musty. To fix it, pour 500 ml distilled vinegar into the machine and
run a 90°C programme.

FOR THE HOB:
Pour a bit of bicarbonate of soda and distilled vinegar on and
around the burners. Leave to sizzle and then wipe off with a
cloth and lukewarm water. (Not suitable for hobs that are
vulnerable to scratches.)

FOR STAINS:
If tea, coffee, limescale or green sediment from flower water, for
example, have left marks, fill the stained vessel with boiling water
and stir in a spoonful of bicarbonate of soda. Cold water will work
too but will take longer, so it's best to leave it to stand overnight.

FOR THE SINK:
If the drains are starting to clog up, it can help to pour 2 tablespoons
of bicarbonate of soda down the drain, followed by 50 ml distilled
vinegar. Leave to work for a while and then flush with hot water.
If the pipes are completely blocked, you will need a more heavy-
duty version: mix 100 ml bicarbonate of soda and 100 ml salt
and pour down the drain. Slowly pour in 100 ml distilled vinegar.
Leave to foam and sizzle for about 15 minutes, then pour in 100 ml
boiling water.

FOR THE KITCHEN SINK:
Rub a squeezed-out lemon over the kitchen sink to get it shiny.
Rinse with warm water.

STUFF

What should you do with the stuff you have cleared out?
Answer: Sell it, swap it with someone or give it away.

The less stuff we surround ourselves with, the easier it is to keep an overview of what we've actually got. Do you sometimes feel that you have to buy something that you probably already have lying around somewhere, just because you can't find it? If so, it's time to go on a stuff diet. Everything will feel a little easier and lighter at home once a few things have been cleared out. And, of course, it's good for the environment not to buy new things that you actually don't need.

If you can also clear things out that you don't use very much, and perhaps rent or borrow instead when you need something, then you are on track for a circular economy, which is the best route for our future. Less stuff = more cooperation!

How should you approach the task to ensure you don't get tired of the clearing out before you've even started? There are a few different tricks you can try, from the KonMari method by Japanese author Marie Kondo (*focusing on what you want to keep, not what you want to throw away*) to the American declutter challenge (*gradually increasing the number of items that you clear out each day*) or look online for storage hacks. They all share strategies with the aim of helping and motivating you to clear things out.

ENOUGH IS THE NEW BLACK

Research looking at, for example, not buying anything for a year and KonMari-style clear-outs has indicated that less consumption often leads to an increase in wellbeing. The conclusion is that we have to start to strive for *enough*. Instead of concentrating on being *more efficient*, we need to focus on the word *less* so that the earth's resources can be enough for everyone, both today and tomorrow.

According to a study, an American power drill is only used for between 6 and 13 minutes during its lifetime. Even if this is a tenfold exaggeration, it's still a complete waste to leave that power drill so unused. All the more reason to think about how we can increase our circular ownership, in other words. How often do you use your power drill?

A NEW STYLE

If you enjoy interior design, you may often feel like redecorating
your home, to create something new and perhaps find a completely
new style. At the same time, of course, you still want to be eco-
friendly. How should you balance these desires? Well, just thinking
about styles is fun in itself. Perhaps you can create a new style from
what you've already got? Try this:

Make a mood board for inspiration. Tear out images from magazines,
save interesting ideas in a folder on your computer. Looking at
pictures is a good way to find the right feel and ambience. Try to
analyse the images that appeal to you. Where is the common thread?
How is the atmosphere created? Is it with a colour range, a style?

Films are another good source of inspiration. Watch a few of your
favourite films: how do the people in them live? Personally, I have a
penchant for French films and that classic Parisian milieu found in
Amélie or *Hunting and Gathering*. Or how about a New York vibe,
like in the films of Woody Allen? What is your favourite film?

SECOND HAND

Once you have found a style it's time to put it into action. Not purchasing anything at all is, as I've mentioned, the best route from an environmental perspective. Borrowing or renting is the next best option. A good alternative is to buy second hand: anything that doesn't involve new production. Buy, but don't forget to sell as well. Sell several items and save up for one special piece that you really want.

SOME GOOD PLACES TO FIND SECOND-HAND
FURNITURE ONLINE:

eBay

Chairish

Facebook Marketplace

Gumtree

Preloved

Shpock

CHARITY ORGANIZATIONS:

Amnesty

British Heart Foundation

British Red Cross

Emmaus

Oxfam

Sue Ryder

Nothing, however, beats a trip to the flea market. It can turn into a little adventure in itself. To make your outing a success you might need to prepare a little. On the next page you'll find my best tips for finding gems at the flea market.

Tips for a good
FLEA MARKET TRIP

- Bring a list of important measurements from home, along with a tape measure or folding ruler to measure any potential buys.
- Arrive in good time.
- Is there a preview? Go to it! Then you will have time to consider what you should bid on.
- If you find something that you really want, buy it straightaway. Otherwise, there is a chance that it will be sold to someone else or you won't be able to find your way back to the stall.
- Otherwise, take your time. Do a few rounds. Usually there are loads of things to look at, so concentrate on a few items at a time.

A LITTLE LESSON IN HAGGLING

Haggling doesn't come naturally to most of us. But at a flea market it's not only allowed, but can even be part of the fun. Here are a few tips:

- If you are buying multiple items, always haggle to try and get a single price for everything. If you can't get the price down, perhaps you can get something extra on top instead.
- Don't appear too keen.
- Ask for time. Say that you will take a walk and think it over. Perhaps the seller will agree to your bid to close the sale. But there is also a chance that the item will be sold to someone else while you are away.
- Only pay what you think the object is worth.

**TO SECURE A BARGAIN
YOU NEED:**

• Eagle eyes.

• A gut feeling.

• A large helping of luck.

• The right moment: either at the
beginning before people get going, or at
the end when people are starting to feel
tired and hungry.

FURTHER READING

Books:

The Balcony Gardener: Creative Ideas for Small Spaces, Isabelle Palmer, 2018, CICO Books

Biophilia: You + Nature + Home, Sally Coulthard, 2020, Kyle Books

How to Break Up with Fast Fashion: A Guilt-Free Guide to Changing the Way You Shop – For Good, Lauren Bravo, 2020, Headline Home

How to Grow Your Dinner Without Leaving the House, Claire Ratinon, 2020, Laurence King Publishing

How to Repair Everything: A Green Guide to Fixing Stuff, Nick Harper, 2020, Michael O'Mara Books

How to Save the World for Free, Natalie Fee, 2021, Laurence King Publishing

100 Ways to Save the World, Johan Tell, 2007, Bonnier Books

Live Green: 52 Steps for a More Sustainable Life, Jen Chillingsworth, 2019, Quadrille Publishing Ltd

A Modern Herbal, Alys Fowler, 2019, Michael Joseph

Waste Not: Make a Big Difference by Throwing Away Less, Erin Rhoads, 2019, Hardie Grant

Government resources:

The Environment Agency
https://www.gov.uk/government/organisations/environment-agency

Keep Britain Tidy
https://www.keepbritaintidy.org/home

Recycle Now
https://www.recyclenow.com/

EQUIVALENT MEASURES

Kilos	Pounds
1	2.2
2	4.5
3	6.6
35	77
74	163
400	882

Litres	US gallons
10	2.6
60	16
100	26.4
150	40
10,000	2642
29,000	7661

Millilitres	US fl. oz.
50	1.7
100	3.4
150	5.1
200	6.8
500	17

°C	°F
−18	−0.4
1.5	34.7
2	35.6
5	41
15	59
16	61
19	66
40	104
60	140
90	194

PICTURE CREDITS

All images were photographed by Ida Magntorn in the following people's homes:

Jessica Barensfeld and Simon Howell, Brooklyn, New York.
www.jebare.com, www.lynnandlawrence.com

Hanna and Peder Berne, Malmö, Sweden.

Johanna Burke, Brooklyn, New York.
burkeandpryde.com

Emily Chalmers, London.
www.emilychalmers.com, instagram: @caravanstyle

Marie Emilsson, Stamnared, Sweden.
instagram: @hakesgard

Ulrika Grönlund, Malmö, Sweden.
www.ulrikagronlund.se, instagram: @ulrikagronlund1

Christina Höglund, Komstad, Sweden.
email: christina@lamafilm.com

Karin Pehrson and Martin Magntorn, Malmö, Sweden.
www.magntorn.com

Lou Rota, London.
instagram: @lou.rota

Catarina Skoglund, Gothenburg, Sweden.
www.annacate.se, instagram: @annacate

Marie Strenghielm, Dalarö, Sweden.
www.strenghielm.se, instagram: @mari_strenghielm

Malene Vetlejord, Malmö, Sweden.

Hanna Welin, St Olof, Sweden.
www.hannawelin.se

THANK YOU

to all of you who helped me make this book!

Those who generously opened your homes and let me come in and photograph.

All the friends on Instagram who contributed inspiration under #mysustainablesunday, an initiative where I asked for ideas and thoughts for this book, and who wanted to give sustainability in the home some extra consideration every Sunday.

Matilde Törnqvist, project manager, Malmö City Council's chemicals strategy, for fact checking.

Maria Ramdén, patient publisher.

My incredibly helpful family: Erik, Mira, Måns and Olle.

www.idamagntorn.se
instagram: @idamagntorn

First published in Sweden by Roos & Tegnér 2020
First published in the United Kingdom in 2022 by
Pavilion
43 Great Ormond Street
London
WC1N 3HZ

ISBN 978-1-91168-211-0

A CIP catalogue record for this book is available from the British Library.

10 9 8 7 6 5 4 3 2 1

Reproduction by Rival Colour Ltd, UK
Printed and bound by Toppan Leefung Ltd, China

www.pavilionbooks.com